Save the Monarch Butterfly

BY KENNETH EADE

OTHER BOOKS BY KENNETH EADE

Brent Marks Legal Thriller Series

A Patriot's Act

Predatory Kill

HOA Wire

Involuntary Spy Espionage Thriller Series

To Russia for Love

An Involuntary Spy (Spy Thriller)

Non-fiction

Bless the Bees: The Pending Extinction of our Pollinators and What You Can Do to Stop It

A, Bee, See: Who are our Pollinators and Why are They in Trouble?

"Love is like a butterfly. It goes where it pleases and pleases where it goes." – **Sri Chinmoy.**

CHAPTER 1: THE KING OF BUTTERFLIES

The Monarch butterfly is thought by many to be the most beautiful of all butterflies, and, if you have ever seen one land on a flower and watched the sun shine through its delicate, exquisite wings, you are reminded of a simply intricate stained glass window. At this point, you will realize that, if the Monarch is not the most beautiful of all butterflies, it certainly counts among them.

The Monarch is also renowned for its incredible annual migration from Mexico to Minnesota and back, over which they travel some 3,000 miles (each way.) Every year hundreds of millions of Monarchs arrive in the ancient Oyamel fir forests of Mihcoacan, Mexico to wait out the winter. Their arrival coincides with the celebration of the "Day of the Dead," and the indigenous Mazahuan people of the region believe that the butterflies are the returning souls of their ancestors. Scientists have marveled at the precision and timing of one of the world's greatest migrations, which takes three generations of Monarchs to complete.

In the Spring, the northern migration begins, and the Monarchs follow the milkweed bloom, laying eggs that will develop into new generations of Monarchs who join the migration. The Monarch only lays its eggs on milkweed. After three to five days, a caterpillar is born, and it consumes the milkweed leaf to survive and to give it chemicals to protect it from predators. When it reaches approximately two inches in length, it forms a chrysalis, in which it makes a spectacular metamorphosis into a butterfly within two weeks.

Sadly, all of this may be coming to an end soon. Because of the proliferation and overuse of pesticides; in particular glyphosate; milkweed, the unique plant necessary for the survival of the species, has been all but obliterated from the migration path.

This has been known for many years, but nothing has been done about it. That is why Monsanto's announcement of March 31, 2015 that it was contributing $3.6 million over the next three years to save the Monarch's natural habitat is ironic, sad, and should be criminal.

According to the US Dept. of Fish and Wildlife, since 1990, 970 million of the billion Monarchs, a total of 90% of the population, have been killed off.

See http://rt.com/usa/230823-monarch-butterflies-monsanto-massacre/ Health and environmental groups have filed a petition to declare the beautiful pollinators endangered and entitled to federal protection.

See http://www.beyondpesticides.org/dailynewsblog/?p=14767 Let us hope that this happens before they all die off, because one thing is for sure – Monsanto's paltry .072% contribution of its five billion per year profits over three years are not going to save them.

This is why the job of saving the Monarch is up to us. If you live in North America, you can do your small part to save these fabulous creatures from extinction and, if you read on, you will learn exactly how to do that.

CHAPTER 2: WHY SHOULD WE CARE ABOUT THE DEMISE OF THE MONARCH?

As a pollinator, the Monarch contributes to pollination, but is not as important a pollinator as the bee. However, it is an indicator species of dangers to our environment; the same dangers which could cause the extinction of larger species, including humans. These include: habitat destruction, lack of biodiversity, climate change and pesticides. The Monarch cannot speak, but it wants you to listen – it is time to stop our dependence on the chemical industrial agricultural system, before it is too late for the Monarch, and for us.

The Monarch's rapid decline points to, and is likely to accelerate, broader environmental degradation. Pollinator population declines are such an important part of the current collapse in biodiversity that seven in ten biologists believe their demise signals an even greater threat to humanity than the global warming which contributes to the decline. These biologists believe we are in the midst of a sixth mass extinction. To put it into perspective, the last mass extinction the earth knew on such a grand scale was the extinction of the dinosaurs about 65 million years ago.

The Chemical-Industrial Agriculture System

Agriculture uses about 70% of the world's fresh water supply. Many food producing countries, such as the United States, China, India, Pakistan, Australia and Spain, are dangerously close to reaching their renewable water limits. The use of fossil water aquifers, which are not being replenished, waste of water resources, leaky irrigation systems and the cultivation of environmentally unfriendly crops, such as corn, are signs of a system which changes the water table, depletes groundwater supplies, and washes pollutants and insecticides into rivers, which destroy freshwater ecosystems, ocean coral reefs and coastal fish breeding grounds.

Pesticides from agriculture can reach water-bearing aquifers below ground from crop fields, seepage of contaminated surface water, spills and leaks, and injection waste material into wells. Many of these pesticides have been given "conditional approval" by the EPA. Therefore, no long term studies have been done as to their safety and their effect on humankind and the environment is unknown.

Dozens of pesticides which we ingest from our food are contributing to major health problems, such as cancer, ADHD, Of these pesticides, chlorpyrifos, one of the most widely used pesticides in American agriculture, has shown up in urine tests of 93% of Americans tested by the CDC. 99% of Americans tested positive for DDT, a pesticide manufactured by Monsanto, which has not been in use since 1972. DDT is a long-lasting persistent organic pollutant that is found in most butter and milk. Girls exposed to DDT are five times more likely to develop breast cancer in their lifetimes.

The same manufacturers of these pesticides, such as Monsanto and Bayer in the United States, and Syngenta in Europe, have genetically engineered plant products to be resistant to their pesticides, which has spawned the use of even more poison, and they have also genetically engineered crops that produce their own biological insecticides, all causing a critical imbalance in the environment at the sake of corporate profits.

This practice, if left uncontrolled, will result in mono-agricultural crops, such as corn, soy and wheat becoming the exclusive crops in the food supply, thus contributing to malnutrition and the eventual the decline of humans as well. The monoculture of non-nutritious products such as soy and corn used as the base for all processed foods have resulted in mass deforestation of essential oxygen producing natural habitats, extinction of species essential to the survival of the biosphere, and the destruction of biodiversity.

As an indicator species, the Monarch is sounding an alarm that we cannot afford to ignore. Industrial agriculture has gone berserk, depending on an extremely high use of pesticides that have caused endemic, long lasting effects on the ecosphere. We must stop acting like we are Gods of our own destiny and respect our mother earth. The planet will be here long after we have destroyed ourselves and caused the mass extinction of most of the species we are familiar with during our time on it. Julia Roberts sums it up wonderfully in this video about the power of nature: http://www.wimp.com/powerful-videos/.

CHAPTER 3: THE CAUSE OF THE MONARCH'S DECLINE

The Monarch butterfly depends upon milkweed to feed and nourish its young. Milkweed is the sole monophagic food source for Monarch larva. Adult butterflies depend on an abundance of flowers to obtain the nectar they need to survive.

What has caused the primary demise of over 90% of the Monarch population is a one-two combination punch of pesticides. Herbicides, and primarily glyphosate, which is the deadly component of Monsanto's Roundup, the most used herbicide in the world, has killed off most of America's milkweed supply. Milkweed used to grow wild on farmland and in between crop fields. Now, due to the prevalence of genetically engineered crops which are resistant to Roundup, farmers can spray their entire fields with Roundup, which eliminates all the weeds. It also eliminates the milkweed, which the Monarchs depend upon to continue their species. Studies have cited an estimated 58% of Midwestern milkweed has disappeared between 1999 and 2010, leading to an 81% decline in the Monarch population. Finally, since glyphosate is systemic, meaning that you cannot wash it off, it goes into your system when you ingest GMO foods.

Glyphosate

A review of hundreds of scientific studies published April 2013 in the scientific journal, *Entropy*, describes the adverse effect of glyphosates on humans, which contribute to gastrointestinal disorders, diabetes, heart disease, obesity, Parkinson's and Alzheimer's disease.

Once called "safer than aspirin," glyphosate's reputation for safety isn't holding up to the scrutiny of independent research. More and more non-industry-funded scientists are finding links between the chemical and all kinds of problems, including cell death, birth defects, miscarriage, low sperm counts, DNA damage, and more recently, destruction of beneficial gut bacteria.

Monsanto (who is also the manufacturer of Agent Orange and DDT) asserts that glyphosate is minimally toxic to humans, but residues of it are found in all of the main foods of the Western diet, which consist primarily of sugar, corn, soy and wheat. Glyphosate's inhibition of cytochrome P450 (CYP) enzymes is an overlooked component of its toxicity to mammals. CYP enzymes play crucial roles in biology, one of which is to detoxify harmful xenobiotics introduced through the diet that are not naturally present in the body. Thus, glyphosate enhances the damaging effects of other food borne chemical residues and environmental toxins. Negative impact is insidious and manifests slowly over time as inflammation damages cellular systems throughout the body. Studies show that CYP enzymes acts synergistically with disruption of the biosynthesis of aromatic amino acids by gut bacteria, as well as the impairment of serum sulfate transport. Consequences are most of the diseases and conditions associated with a Western diet, which include gastrointestinal disorders, obesity, diabetes, heart disease, depression, autism, infertility, cancer and Alzheimer's disease.

Since chemical companies invented genetically engineered seeds designed to withstand heavy sprayings of glyphosate, global use of Roundup and related weed killers has jumped to nearly 900 million pounds annually. That is due to the fact that, since the crops are engineered to be resistant to Roundup, it can be sprayed on the entire field, not just on the weeds, making it much easier for farmers to manage weed kills. Glyphosate is a systemic chemical, meaning once sprayed, it travels up inside of the plants that people and animals eat and they consume the glyphosate as well as the nutrients in the plants. As more farm fields have converted to GMO crops, federal regulators have quietly allowed an increase in the levels of glyphosate allowed in your food, something from which we should see tragic long term consequences.

Neonicotinoids

Neonicotinoid insecticides are a new class of systemic, neurotoxic pesticides that has been shown by a USDA study to be particularly toxic to Monarchs and other pollinators. Neonicotinoids have rapidly taken over the global insecticide market since their introduction in the 1990s. These neonicotinoids, such as *imidacloprid, clothianidin* and *thiametoxam*, are used as seed treatments in hundreds of crops from corn to almonds, as well as in lawn care and flea products. The insecticides are routinely applied directly to the seed, and the developing plant absorbs them and expresses them in its pollen and nectar, thus causing a lethal problem for pollinators. Moreover, they persist in the soil for approximately 12 years, infecting any new plants that may be planted to replace them.

Italy, Germany, France and the European Union itself have taken action against neonicotinoids to protect their pollinators (and the European Union has already been sued by Syngenta and Bayer for this action), but in the United States, where science is mostly funded by the industries who benefit from the insecticides, only prophylactic labeling has been enacted by the EPA, while at the same time paradoxically approving new neonicotinoid insecticides for the market. This is nothing new. Around the same time, French beekeepers succeeded in banning neonicotinoids, the EPA under the Clinton administration permitted pesticides which were previously banned, including imidacloprid. In 2004, the Bush Administration reduced regulations further and pesticide applications increased.

Virtually all of the genetically engineered (GMO) Bt corn grown in the U.S. is treated with neonicotinoids and a 2012 study found high levels of clothianidin in pneumatic planter exhaust. In the study, it was found that the insecticide was present in the soil of unplanted fields nearby those planted with Bt corn and also on dandelions growing near those fields.

Features of Neonicotinoid Pesticides

• Persistent in soil and water soluble.

• Systemic pesticides applied at the root (as seed coating or drench) & then taken up through the plant's vascular system to be expressed in pollen, nectar & guttation droplets from which bees then forage and drink.

• Cannot be washed off.

• Nicotine-like, neurotoxic insecticides that bind to nicotinic acetylcholine receptors in insects' brains. (Bees are more susceptible to these insecticides because they have more of these receptors, as well as more learning and memory genes, and fewer genes for detoxification.)

• Widely used on more than 140 crop varieties, as well as on termites, flea treatments, lawns & gardens.

• Fastest-growing class of synthetic pesticides in history.

Strong correlations are found in the rise of neonicotinoid pesticides and Colony Collapse Disorder, as well as plummeting wildlife populations in areas where the chemicals are heavily used. Outbreaks of infectious diseases in many wildlife populations, including fish, amphibians, bats, and birds, coincide on a temporal and geographic scale with the emerging use of the pesticides. Non-target insects are also being wiped out, depriving wildlife of a food source.

These pesticides are so lethal because they are designed to disrupt the central nervous system. While very effective on pests, they are not specific to pests and appear to work on all animal life forms from invertebrates to mammals.

Researchers hypothesize that neonicotinoid pesticides have another sub lethal effect of damaging the immune system of a variety of wildlife, making them more susceptible to infectious disease outbreaks that correlate with use of the pesticide. Neonicotinoids persist in the environment, and do not break down quickly. These pesticides are typically applied to crop seeds. The chemical is ingested into the plant and travels to the growing shoots and flowers, where it is toxic to anything that eats any part of it. The chemicals are also applied as a soil treatment. When it rains, the chemicals get washed into aquatic ecosystems.

CHAPTER 4: HOW TO SAVE THE MONARCH BUTTERFLY

In May 2015, President Barack Obama revealed a national strategy to mitigate honey bee loss, increase the Monarch butterfly population and restore their habitats. The strategy essentially consists of rehabilitating butterfly habitats and planting milkweed alongside Interstate 35, a highway that goes from the Texas-Mexico border to Duluth, Minnesota. That would be a great idea if butterflies used freeways, which, of course, they do not.

While this should mitigate some population losses and perhaps build back some of their numbers, the plan fails to address the fatal effect that glyphosate and neonicotinoid pesticides have had on the Monarch, and fails to propose a ban of these pesticides. The reason why is that the agro-chemical industry is heavily invested in these environmentally toxic chemicals. The market for glyphosate was $5.46 billion in 2012, and is expected to reach $8.79 billion by 2019. This means a virtual elimination of all milkweed, except, of course, the corridor along I-35. Neonicotinoids represent one-third of the global insecticide market.

Reduce the use of pesticides

The first step you can take in saving the Monarch butterfly is to eliminate foods which are grown using (and contain) neonicotinoids and glyphosate, using these simple steps:

• **Buy organic foods:** Roundup and other chemical pesticides and fertilizers are banned for use in organic agriculture. Instead, organic farmers focus on building healthy soil to support the growth of healthy plants. To find local sustainable farmers, try this site: http://Localharvest.org.

• **Avoid genetically engineered foods.** Avoid corn, which in the United States, is 90% GMO, and all corn products, including high fructose corn syrup (HFCS), which is present in most processed foods and drinks.

• **Avoid all processed foods.** The main glyphosate-laden foods that wind up in the food supply are corn, soy, and canola. Since these ingredients readily wind up in about 80 percent of processed foods, eating more whole foods (or choosing organic processed foods) can help lower your exposure to the chemical.

Multi-billion dollar corporations cannot survive without their ultimate consumer – and that is you! If an overwhelming number of us avoid the above-referenced foods, three things will happen:

• **Prices of organics will go down.** If more organics are demanded by the public, there will be more grown and offered in supermarkets, and the prices of them will go down, due to the increased supply.

• **Health costs will go down.** Better nutrition and poison-free food means that, not only will your health improve, but there will be less dependence on pharmaceutical solutions to nutrition-caused health problems.

• **Pesticide use will drop, instead of increase.** Not only will your efforts be saving the butterflies, the bees, and yourselves, if more of us avoid these toxic products, the system will have to change to adapt to consumer demand.

Of course, the above scenario of a rosy, healthy future is only if many of us come together in numbers to produce a paradigm shift in the way our food is brought to the table. But, it starts with you.

Plant Milkweed

The second step to saving the Monarch butterfly is to plant milkweed in your own backyard or garden. Milkweed is a wild plant, but you can obtain seeds for a small donation or even for free from many organizations. These include:

1. *Live Monarch*: https://www.livemonarch.com/free-milkweed-seeds.htm
2. Monarch Butterfly Garden: https://monarchbutterflygarden.net/milkweed-plant-seed-resources/

Milkweed seeds can also be purchased obtained from local nurseries.

Once you have planted milkweed, a good idea is to pass along the seeds to someone else. This is a good site for learning how to save milkweed seeds: http://www.ourhabitatgarden.org/creatures/milkweed-growing.html

Organizations such as Monarch Watch will take the seeds you don't re-use to plant new milkweed and put them to use where they are most needed. You can find out how to send them seeds by visiting their website at http://www.monarchwatch.org/, which is also a wonderful resource of information on these beautiful creatures.

Act politically

Finally, acting politically is a good way to help the Monarch, and it is as easy as punching a button on your smart phone in between texting, taking selfies, and watching cat videos. Here is how you do it:

1. **Contact your representatives**. Your representatives may be bought and paid for by big agriculture, but they depend on your vote to stay in office. Writing an email to your Congressman and Senators takes just a few minutes. If you like, you can cut and paste this message:

    "I recently read a book called, *Save the Monarch Butterfly,* which pointed out the deadly effects that glyphosate and neonicotinoid pesticides have had on our pollinators. In particular, the Monarch Butterfly's numbers have been reduced by over 90%, due mostly to glyphosate wiping out milkweed in North America that they depend on during their migration. I call upon you, my elected representative, to call for a ban on these toxic chemicals in Congress, and to pressure the EPA to ban them."

    The following resources are websites where you can obtain the email addresses of your representatives:

    U.S. Senators:
    http://www1.umn.edu/humanrts/peace/senate.html

    U.S. Congressmen: http://www.contactingthecongress.org/

    President of the United States:
    https://www.whitehouse.gov/contact/

2. **Sign a Petition.** Groups such as these are circulating petitions asking the government and governmental agencies and others to take action to save the Monarch. A simple Google search will reveal which petitions are now active. One click of a button and you will add your name to the petition, joining your voice with thousands of others or even start your own petition:

    www.thepetitionsite.com

    www.sumofus.org

    www.credomobilize.com

www.petitions.moveon.org

www.change.org

www.care2.com

Like Neil Armstrong said when he landed on the moon, your one small step forward in helping the Monarch butterfly can be part of a giant leap forward for all of us.

REFERENCES

Chapter 1

http://articles.mercola.com/sites/articles/archive/2015/01/31/glyphosate-monarch-butterflies.aspx

http://www.monarch-butterfly.com/

http://www.ecolifefoundation.org/programs/mexico-monarch-butterfly-program/

http://www.mlmp.org/results/findings/pleasants_and_oberhauser_2012_milkweed_loss_in_ag_fields.pdf

http://news.monsanto.com/press-release/giving/national-fish-and-wildlife-foundation-and-monsanto-announce-commitment-help-mon

http://rt.com/usa/230823-monarch-butterflies-monsanto-massacre/

http://www.beyondpesticides.org/dailynewsblog/?p=14767

http://umaine.edu/signs-of-the-seasons/indicator-species/monarch/fact-sheet/

http://www.opednews.com/articles/Monsanto-murders-almost-a-by-Kenneth-G-Eade-Butterflies_Extinction_Glyphosate_Monarch-Butterfly-150401-73.html

http://www.fs.fed.us/wildflowers/pollinators/documents/Monarch_Butterfly.pdf

http://michiganradio.org/post/whats-driving-drop-monarch-butterfly-numbers

Chapter 2

http://www.independentsciencenews.org/news/new-research-links-neonicotinoid-pesticides-to-monarch-butterfly-declines/

http://www.kare11.com/story/news/local/monarchs/2015/05/11/monarch-mission-butterfly-population-rapidly-declining/27139361/

http://wwf.panda.org/what_we_do/footprint/agriculture/impacts/water_use/

https://water.usgs.gov/edu/pesticidesgw.html

http://www.panna.org/issues/food-agriculture/pesticides-on-food

http://www.opednews.com/articles/It-is-time-to-abandon-the-by-Kenneth-G-Eade-Agriculture_Agriculture_Agriculture-And-Forestry_Bayer-141216-942.html

Chapter 3

http://healthimpactnews.com/2014/is-glyphosate-responsible-for-your-health-problems/

http://www.mdpi.com/1099-4300/15/4/1416

http://permaculturenews.org/2012/11/01/why-glyphosate-should-be-banned-a-review-of-its-hazards-to-health-and-the-environment/

http://www.realfarmacy.com/weapon-of-mass-wildlife-destruction-neonicotinoid-pesticides-at-the-root-of-global-wildlife-declines/#zolt7TI2zDQF08wd.99

http://www.independentsciencenews.org/news/new-research-links-neonicotinoid-pesticides-to-monarch-butterfly-declines/

http://www.onearth.org/earthwire/monarch-butterfly-glyphosphate-neonicotinoids

http://www.bioscienceresource.org/?attachment_id=5007

http://www.iucn.org/news_homepage/?16025/Systemic-Pesticides-Pose-Global-Threat-to-Biodiversity-And-Ecosystem-Services

http://onlinelibrary.wiley.com/doi/10.1111/1365-2664.12111/abstract;jsessionid=358222E3D063303865EAA83718714B29.f04t04?deniedAccessCustomisedMessage=&userIsAuthenticated=false

Chapter 4

http://sustainablepulse.com/2014/08/21/glyphosate-sales-boom-powers-global-biotech-industry/

http://www.ncbi.nlm.nih.gov/pmc/articles/PMC4284366/

Photographic credits:

Chapter 4: Credit: David Wagner